CODING WITH ROBOTICS

Express!

BY KYLIE BURNS

BELLWETHER MEDIA • MINNEAPOLIS, MN

Express!

Imagination comes alive in Express!
Transform the everyday into the fresh and
new, discover ways to stir up flavor and
excitement, and experiment with new
ideas and materials. Express! makerspace
books: where your next creative
adventure begins!

This edition first published in 2024 by Bellwether Media, Inc.

No part of this publication may be reproduced in whole or in part without written permission of the publisher.
For information regarding permission, write to Bellwether Media, Inc., Attention: Permissions Department,
6012 Blue Circle Drive, Minnetonka, MN 55343.

Library of Congress Cataloging-in-Publication Data

LC record for Coding with Robotics available at: https://lccn.loc.gov/2023022002

Editors: Sarah Eason and Christina Leaf
Illustrator: Eric Smith
Series Design: Brittany McIntosh
Graphic Designer: Paul Myerscough

Printed in the United States of America, North Mankato, MN.

TABLE OF CONTENTS _ □ X

Coding is **communicating** with computers so they can perform tasks. When we communicate with other humans, we speak a language that the other person understands. Coding is a way to give **commands** to computers in a language that they understand called **code**.

These robots use code to follow step-by-step instructions, but they cannot make decisions on their own.

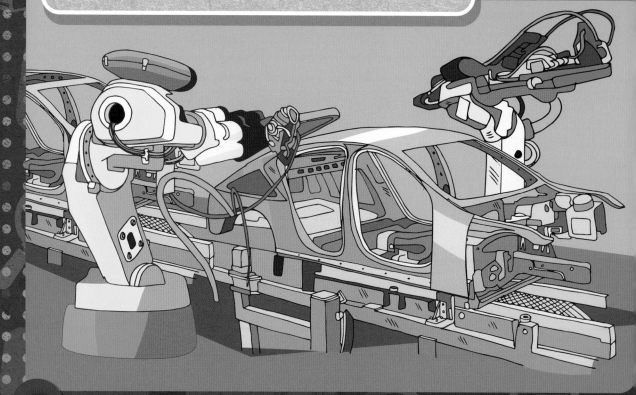

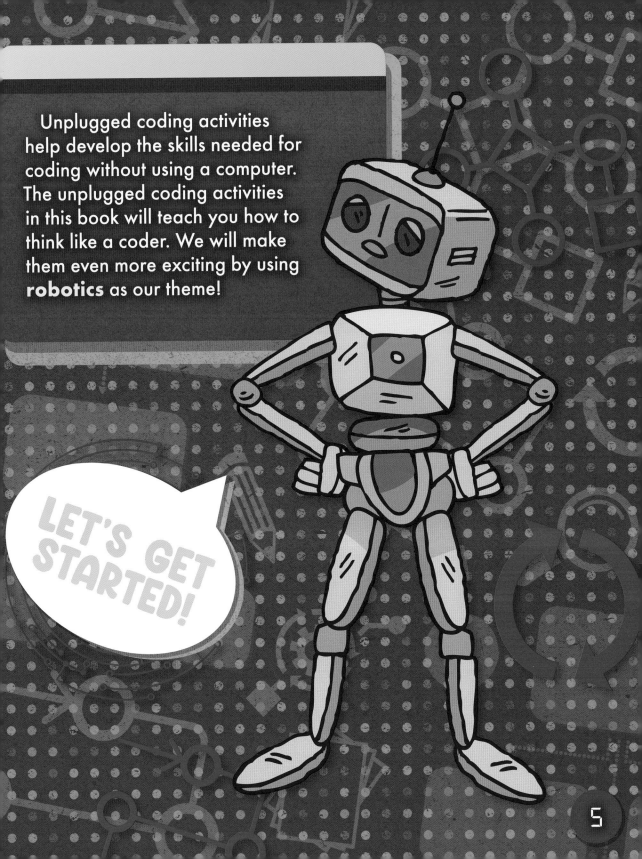

Unplugged coding activities help develop the skills needed for coding without using a computer. The unplugged coding activities in this book will teach you how to think like a coder. We will make them even more exciting by using **robotics** as our theme!

LET'S GET STARTED!

ROBOT CLEANER! _ □ X

Coders must include step-by-step instructions when writing code so the computer can correctly carry out a task. However, some tasks require many steps, and that creates a very long program. One way to reduce the lines of code is to build a **function**. A function is a named group of coding steps that can be used over and over.

YOU WILL NEED: _ □ X

- a pencil
- paper

In this activity, you will use functions to tell a robot to clean your room! You must name the function for each task. For example, if you want the robot to pick up your socks, you could name the function "stinkysocks." Follow the numbered steps for an example of "stinkysocks."

LET'S TRY IT OUT!

1 Find sock on floor.

2 Travel to sock.

3

Reach out arm and grab sock.

4

Lift sock.

5

Travel to laundry basket.

6

Release and drop sock in basket.

You have your first function! Now try creating another for making your bed called "makethebed." How would you order the steps? Test it by making your bed and writing down each step in the correct order.

TURN THE PAGE TO SEE HOW YOU DID!

DID YOU KNOW?

A function can be used many times in a code. The coder just includes the function's name, and the computer knows which steps to take!

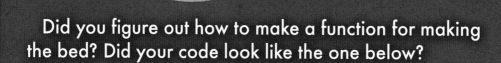

Did you figure out how to make a function for making the bed? Did your code look like the one below?

1. Move to bed.
2. Reach out and grab sheet.
3. Pull sheet toward pillow.
4. Tuck sheet sides under mattress.
5. Reach out and grab blanket.
6. Pull blanket toward pillow.
7. Smooth blanket out.

To write a code to clean your room, you could use the functions "stinkysocks" and "makethebed."

1. Move around room.
2. "stinkysocks"
3. Move around room.
4. "makethebed"

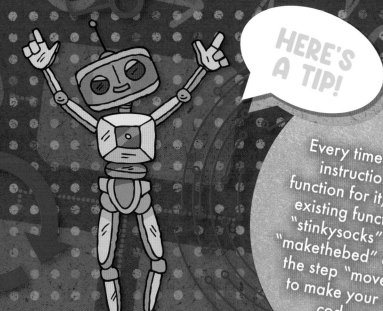

HERE'S A TIP!

Every time you see a repeat instruction, try making a function for it, or include it in an existing function. The function "stinkysocks" and the function "makethebed" could also include the step "move around room" to make your room cleaning code even shorter.

CODING CHALLENGE! _ □ X

Play this game with a friend. One person is the coder, and one is the robot.

You Will Need:
- paper
- a pencil
- 12 plastic cups

The coder must write down the steps for building something with the plastic cups, such as a tower or a pyramid. Next, the coder identifies any steps that repeat and can be put into functions. On a separate sheet of paper, they should write each function with the steps underneath. Then, the coder rewrites the code on a new sheet of paper using functions for any actions that repeat. The robot takes the sheet with the rewritten code and the sheet with the functions and tries to follow them exactly to see if they can do what is asked. If the robot fails, the coder must correct the code. The robot then tries again. Take turns being the coder and the robot.

HANDY ROBOT   _ □ X

Sometimes, coders create **variables** for storing pieces of information called **values**. The variable groups the values by something they have in common. For example, think of a robot that is programmed to pick things up. The variable is named "grab," and the value can be any item the coder decides. If several items are going to be grabbed, the value, or item, can change, but the variable, "grab," remains the same.

In this activity, you will make your own robot hand with a grab variable that you can use to pick up different values!

LET'S TRY IT OUT!

1
Trace your hand onto the cardboard with your fingers slightly spread out.

2
Cut out the hand.

3

Draw lines on each finger that show the joints where the fingers bend.

4

Fold the fingers on each of the lines, toward the palm of the hand.

5

Cut pieces of straws to fit into each section on the fingers. Tape them down.

6

Tape longer pieces of straws to the palm of the hand.

7

Attach a bead to the end of each piece of yarn. Thread the other end of the yarn through the straw pieces. Start at the end of each finger and thread toward the palm.

8

Tie the ends of the yarn into a knot, and pull them to make your robot fingers move.

9

Try out your hand by choosing some items to be values for your robot to pick up.

TURN THE PAGE FOR MORE ON VARIABLES!

CHECK IT OUT!

How did your robot hand turn out? Was it difficult or easy to make? Did the fingers move well? How many values did you manage to pick up using the variable "grab"?

HERE'S A TIP!

Think like a coder! See if you can find examples of variables and values in your life! For example, one variable might be tasks for a robot helper. Values could be vacuuming, dusting, or picking up toys!

CODING CHALLENGE!

_ □ X

You Will Need:
- plain stickers or pieces of masking tape
- a marker
- a timer

Try this challenge with at least six friends. Choose someone to be the coder. Have the other players stand shoulder to shoulder, facing away from the coder. The coder places a sticker or piece of tape with the number 1, 2, or 3 onto each person's back, so they cannot see it. The variable is the team number, and the values are the team members. The coder gives the instruction that the values, or players, must group themselves by variable, or number, without speaking. The coder then sets the timer for 2 minutes. When the game begins, players with the same number on their sticker must find each other. After time is up, see how many people were able to find their team.

CHANGING GEARS   _ □ X

Why is programming a robot to climb the stairs two at a time helpful? If you said, "to get to the top with fewer steps," you are right! The robot could climb the stairs one at a time. But making it take two stairs at a time can get the robot up the stairs more quickly. In coding, this is known as **optimization**.

YOU WILL NEED: _ □ X

- sidewalk chalk
- a single die
- paper
- a pencil
- an outdoor area with a flat surface for drawing

In this game, you will use optimization to help your robot! Play with a friend. You are on a mission to collect gears and springs to optimize your robot. One person is the coder, and the other is the collector.

LET'S SPRING INTO ACTION!

1

Draw a 6x6 square grid on pavement using sidewalk chalk.

14

2

Draw two gears, two springs, and seven red Xs in different squares on the grid.

gear

spring

3

Draw a green circle in a corner square for the start. On the opposite side of the grid in a corner square, write an R for robot. This will be the finish.

4

The coder rolls the die and tells the collector directions for where to step. For example, if a 2 is rolled, the collector moves two steps in any direction the coder chooses. The coder should write down each step on the paper. The goal is to collect all of the springs and gears in the fewest steps possible. Be sure to avoid any square with an X. If the collector steps on an X, they must start over.

When the collector reaches the finish, they can look over the paper copy of the route to see if there is a way to optimize it even more. Could there be fewer steps? If so, the collector writes down the new, optimized route. Then the collector and the coder switch places, with the collector instructing the coder to follow the new, optimized route.

TURN THE PAGE TO KEEP OPTIMIZING!

CHECK IT OUT!

How did the activity go? Was it difficult to optimize the route? What could you do differently next time?

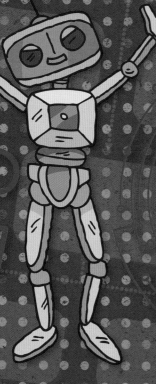

HERE'S A TIP!

Think like a coder and find ways to optimize things you do every day. Start with the goal, and then write down the steps to achieve it. Finally, test it out. Look for ways to combine steps or other ways to improve your optimized task.

In order to optimize, a coder must get rid of unnecessary steps. Try this robot-building challenge with a friend and test your optimization skills.

You Will Need:
- building blocks (such as LEGO bricks)
- a piece of cardboard
- a table or desktop surface

You will start as the coder, and your friend will be the computer. Sit opposite each other at the table or desk. Make sure each side has the exact same blocks to work with. Fold the piece of cardboard so that it acts as a wall and blocks your friend's view of your side. Build a robot out of the blocks. Then, give instructions one step at a time to the computer to see if your friend can build a robot that is exactly the same.

Try to think about ways to optimize. Are there instructions you could group as functions, such as the steps for building the robot's legs? Try making a "buildleg" function and teaching it to your friend. How does it change the instructions that you give? Take turns being the coder and the computer.

DID YOU KNOW?

Robots that look and act like people are called humanoid robots. That is because they are programmed to perform tasks in the same way humans do, with optimization!

THINK LIKE A ROBOT! _ □ X

Like coding, **critical thinking** involves **analyzing** and breaking down problems into smaller steps that can be individually fixed or improved.

Play this critical thinking game with a partner. Take turns as the coder and the robot.

YOU WILL NEED: _ □ X

- mini colored sticky notes in four colors
- a black marker
- colored markers or crayons in the same colors as the sticky notes
- a game piece, such as a small toy car
- index cards
- paper
- a pencil
- a timer

LET'S TRY IT OUT!

1

First, the coder makes a 5x5 grid pattern by placing 25 sticky notes on the floor in a color pattern of their choice.

18

2

Then, the coder colors a mini map of the same grid pattern on five index cards by using the markers in similar colors.

3

The coder uses arrows to draw a different path from start to end on each of the index cards, using the black marker. There should be no more than seven steps in the path. The coder changes the path and the start/end spots on each of the five cards.

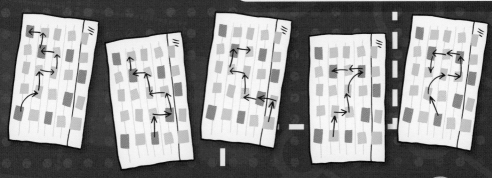

4

The robot picks up one of the cards and has one minute to memorize the path. When the minute is up, the robot gives the card back to the coder. The robot tries to move the game piece along the memorized path on the sticky note grid. Repeat Step 4 with all five index cards.

5

Each time the game piece follows the path exactly to the end, the robot earns a point. Take turns being the coder and the robot. The player with the most points at the end of the game wins!

DID YOU KNOW?

The central processing unit (CPU) is like the brain of a robot. It helps the robot to perform specific actions based on data.

TURN THE PAGE FOR MORE CRITICAL THINKING!

What happened when you tried to memorize the coder's instruction card? Were you able to follow the correct paths? Was there a critical thinking approach that helped you make choices and win points? What would you change now that you have tried the game?

HERE'S A TIP!

Critical thinking skills make coding easier. They include grouping similar patterns or finding things that are alike.

CODING CHALLENGE!

_ ☐ **X**

You Will Need:
- a flat surface to work on
- 7 pieces of paper (cut to any size) in a variety of shapes, such as squares, rectangles, and circles
- scissors

Can you create a paper robot with just seven pieces of paper? Think about how you would use each piece and how you would place them on the flat surface. What size are your pieces? How does that affect where or how the pieces are used to achieve your goal? Use critical thinking skills to complete the challenge. Take a picture of your paper robot when you have finished!

I HOPE YOU ENJOYED UNPLUGGED CODING!

GLOSSARY

_ □ **X**

analyzing—looking carefully at something to understand how it works and its important parts

code—instructions for a computer

commands—specific instructions to complete a task

communicating—sharing knowledge or information

critical thinking—a way of thinking that involves breaking down a problem or information and results in a logical conclusion

function—a part of a code that can be used over and over

optimization—a way to improve a code so that it works more quickly and takes up less space in a computer

robotics—the technology dealing with the making and operating of robots

values—pieces of information in a code; values are often part of a variable.

variables—parts of a code that store information; variables contain related values.

AT THE LIBRARY

Lang, Taylor. *Critical Thinking Activities for Kids.* Emeryville, Calif.: Rockridge Press, 2021.

Noll, Elizabeth. *Factory Robots.* Minneapolis, Minn.: Bellwether Media, 2018.

Prottsman, Kiki. *How to Be a Coder.* New York, N.Y.: DK Publishing, 2019.

ON THE WEB

FACTSURFER

Factsurfer.com gives you a safe, fun way to find more information.

1. Go to www.factsurfer.com.

2. Enter "coding with robotics" into the search box and click 🔍.

3. Select your book cover to see a list of related content.

INDEX ☐ X